BK 735.094   R692H
HOMAGE TO RODIN
                              /RODIN, AUG
    1967   .00   FV

3000 128907 30010
St. Louis Community College

400

W9-DIU-113

735.094 R692h   FV
RODIN
  HOMAGE TO RODIN   4.00

JUNIOR COLLEGE DISTRICT
of St. Louis-St. Louis County
LIBRARY
7508 Forsyth Blvd.
St. Louis, Missouri 63105

Homage to Rodin

Gift of B. Gerald Cantor to the Los Angeles County Museum of Art.

Homage to **Rodin**

Collection of *B. Gerald Cantor*

Los Angeles County Museum of Art   1967

Copyright 1967 by the Los Angeles County Museum of Art.
Library of Congress Catalog Card Number: 67-31131
No part of this catalog may be reproduced in any form without written
permission from the publisher.

5,700 copies of *Homage to Rodin*, have been printed in November, 1967
for the Los Angeles County Museum of Art on the occasion of the exhibition.
Typography by Vernon Simpson Typographers Inc., Los Angeles.
Monotype Centaur and Arrighi by Mackenzie & Harris, Inc., San Francisco.
Catalog design by Robert R. Overby.
Photography by Edward Cornachio.

Homage to Rodin

Los Angeles County Museum of Art,

November 14, 1967 - January 7, 1968

The Museum of Fine Arts, Houston,

January 31, 1968 - March 3, 1968

The Brooklyn Museum, New York,

May 13, 1968 - August 25, 1968

Virginia Museum of Fine Arts, Richmond,

September 16, 1968 - October 20, 1968

California Palace of the Legion of Honor, San Francisco,

November 21, 1968 - January 5, 1969

Contents

Foreword

Collecting is a creative act. The serious collector selects and rejects, no less than the artist, until he finds the values which are meaningful to him. He tirelessly adds, subtracts and modifies to give the collection its mature character. The result is an entity quite distinct from its components—the creation of the collector. Its statement about the collector and his world is often strikingly different from that made by any single work of art it includes.

A tiny hand by Rodin is wondrous in that it embodies the surging energy of a whole being; a collection of Rodin reveals that vital energy as a natural force common to all living beings, as infinite in its outward expression as there are individuals and moments of life. To form a Rodin collection is a task as endless as the variety of the master. It demands a personal commitment to the artist's aim as unflagging as that of the scholar or the missionary. Such a commitment has become part of the nature of B. Gerald Cantor.

Mr. Cantor's preoccupation with Rodin began fortuitously and developed slowly. One Sunday afternoon in the Spring of 1945 walking through the Metropolitan Museum he came upon the first sculpture of Rodin he had ever seen, the *Hand of God*. With the suddenness of revelation, he found a consonance with the artist which he has never lost. A year and a half later he acquired his first Rodin sculpture, another version of the *Hand of God*. During the next decade Mr. Cantor was more concerned with building his collection of early twentieth century painting than with sculpture, but the magnetic attraction of Rodin persisted. Then in the late fifties he bought *Eternal Spring* and *The Kiss*. His commitment was made. Rodin was unescapable.

Mr. Cantor now gave countless hours to the study of the Rodin literature, to museum visits wherever Rodins are found, and to seeking sources of acquisition. He haunted the Musée Rodin. At this juncture, he met Mme. Cécile Goldscheider who became his cherished friend and advisor. The collection grew apace as Mr. Cantor added to the sculptures of broad popular appeal with which he had begun, objects which require deeper understanding and more continuous involvement.

It is in these latter works that one might find the closest agreement with Mr. Cantor's individuality: physically powerful, charged with energy, restless for new challenges, emotionally volatile but with deep loyalties and human concern. For Mr. Cantor like Rodin, the world is seen in transition, life is perpetual flux.

In assembling his collection, Mr. Cantor has restricted the scale of his sculptures to that with which he can live intimately in his home and office. While the bronzes vary in date over the past two decades, they have all been authenticated by the Musée Rodin as having been cast from original Rodin plasters and as being within the total number, usually twelve, established as the maximum for each work.

As an American collector of Rodin, Mr. Cantor is heir to a distinguished tradition which includes the dancer Loïe Fuller, whose collection was presented at the National Arts Club in New York in 1903 as the first sizeable Rodin exhibition in America; Thomas Fortune Ryan, who donated a number of Rodin sculptures to the Metropolitan Museum of Art between 1910 and 1913; Samuel Hill, whose collection distinguishes the Maryville, Washington, Museum of Fine Arts which

he founded in 1922; Jules E. Mastbaum who presented
the Rodin Museum and its entire collection to the
city of Philadelphia in the late twenties; and Mrs. Alma
de Bretteville Spreckles of San Francisco who gave
her superb collection to the California Palace of the
Legion of Honor between 1932 and 1950.

Mr. Cantor has been a consistent patron of the Los
Angeles County Museum of Art, having donated twelve
paintings by noted nineteenth and twentieth century artists from Puvis de Chavannes to Picasso,
Kirchner and Beckmann over the past fifteen years.
His most recent contribution is the 50¼ inch bronze
of the mighty striding Balzac, in this exhibition,
considered by Rodin scholars to be the finest sculpture
in the entire series of preliminary studies for the
Balzac monument.

I would like to express our gratitude first of all to
Mr. Cantor not only for lending the paramount objects
from his collection, but for his having spared no
effort, time or trips to Europe to forestall disappoint-
ments; to Mme. Cécile Goldscheider, Conservateur
of the Musée Rodin, for her generous cooperation and
her provision of both the introductory essay and the
catalog notes, and to Mlle. Edith Lionne, her assistant;
to Mr. Hal Skolnik for being of assistance in whatever strange place he was needed; to Ed Cornachio for
his perception and infinite patience, in French and
English, in photographing the collection; to James
Monte for coordinating the exhibition and catalog, and
installing the show; and to Ellen Landis for pre-
paring the bibliography and translating the notes.

Kenneth Donahue, *Director*
Los Angeles County Museum of Art

Introduction

Auguste Rodin, honored and acknowledged by American collectors and museums during his lifetime, never crossed the Atlantic although he was invited to do so many times. After his death the fervor of the new world's admiration did not subside. Succeeding generations of Americans as well as Europeans have been particularly interested in Rodin's lesser known works, thus broadening the field of selection. The B. Gerald Cantor collection not only typifies the recurrent interest in Rodin's work, but surveys little known areas within the master's prolific working life. The Cantor collection is certainly the most important private collection in the United States.

The eternal, classic character of great sculpture is represented in this collection by such pieces as: *The Age of Bronze, St. John the Baptist,* and *The Kiss.* The artist's boldness bursts forth in both conception and form in his sculptural studies for the monumental *Gates of Hell.* Studies for the Balzac monument opened new perspectives for contemporary sculpture. The taste of our times emphasizes the importance of improvisation of design as well as its consistent development towards a preconceived conception of form. In many cases improvisation, even with the imperfections of a fleeting inspiration, is preferred to a totally resolved execution. The selections Mr. Cantor has made from Rodin's sculptures affords visual evidence of the diversity and force within the work of the French master.

Rodin, when he finally received recognition after years of hardship and struggle, said, "Up to the age of 50 I suffered all the discomforts of poverty. I have always lived like a workman, but because work has brought me happiness, I have been able to endure everything." *Work* is the key to Rodin's philosophy and explains his immense production. It incessantly recurs in his statements and is remarked upon in a letter to Rodin by Rainier Marie-Rilke written on September 11, 1902: ". . . It is not only for the sake of study that I came to see you, it was to ask you 'How one should live?' and you answered me 'working'. I feel what you mean is that working is living without smiling." Rilke, who arrived at Rodin's studio to write a monograph on the artist and remained to become his secretary, knew first-hand of the sculptor's indefatigable, and at times tyrannical, will to work. Antoine Bourdelle's depiction of *Rodin at Work* affords visual testimony to the poet's words, and depicts Rodin in a ferociously attentive working attitude.

Auguste Rodin was born in Paris in 1840 and was the second child in the family. In his youth he was a mediocre student, a fact which later in life bothered the artist and he did, in fact, remedy by intensive reading. In 1854 he entered the Imperial School of Drawing and Mathematics to study drawing. He was to discover, one year later, his intense affinity for sculptural modelling. In the period which followed Rodin foresaw his true vocation: sculpture. In 1857, having completed his studies, he hoped to continue his training at the Beaux-Arts Academy, but his father, anxious of the uncertain future befalling artists, sought the advice of a then famous sculptor, Hippolyte Maindron. The artist's judgment was favorable; the young Rodin should study at the Beaux-Arts, which alone could lead to official recognition of his talent. Three consecutive failures in the admittance competition did not discourage Rodin; his dedication to a personal ideal disallowed discouragement. Because family means were extremely limited, Rodin sought employment with decorators in order to earn a living. His work in collaboration with these firms went unnoticed and was lost in the collective nature of the enterprises. No work of this time is left with the exception of some drawings and oil portraits.

The equilibrium of his emotional life was destroyed by the death of his sister in 1862. He went through a mystical crisis and entered the Novitiate of the Congregation of the Holy Sacrament. Having obtained the authorization to model from his Superior, Rodin made the first portrait dated with certainty, that of the *Reverend Father Eymard,* founder of the Congregation. A sensitive and highly intelligent man, Father Eymard managed to convince the young novice that his vocation was that of a sculptor and not of a priest. His bust of 1863 exhibits the talent of an artist already able to capture the character and likeness of the model. After a few months of retreat and meditation in the convent, Rodin returned to his family and resumed his work in a spirit made mature by his ordeal.

In 1864, Rodin worked on the façade of the Goblins Theater in Paris, where two of his winged figures still adorn the outside loge. In the same year he met a young woman, Marie-Rose Beuret. She who was to one day write, "I live only to obey you," modestly took her place in an existence which could not blossom and develop without the presence of a woman. The couple moved into a converted stable, doubling as a studio, where Marie-Rose posed for the struggling young sculptor. With the exception of some portraits, busts in terra cotta characterized by minute rendering of garment details, we do not possess works from this period. The sculpture entitled *Mask of the Man with the Broken Nose* and presented to the Salon in 1864 is an exception. The head band holding back the rebellious locks gives to the face the nobility of an ancient, but was rejected because it contradicted the tastes of the Salon jurors.

Collaboration with Carrier-Belleuse, which began in 1864, improved the lot of the artist. A student of David d'Angers, Albert Carrier de Belleuse had the greatest reputation among the sculptor-decorators of the Second Empire and the beginning of the Republic. Because of large and important orders he established a production system for carrying out the commissions. Teams of artists and craftsmen carried out the preparation, roughing-out and casting of the projects. He was attracted by the talent evinced in Rodin's work, realized the use to which he could put it and went so far as to put his signature on pieces modelled by Rodin.

The military defeat of France in 1870, soon followed by the fall of the Empire and the siege of Paris, forced the Parisian sculpture yards to close. The unemployed French artists sought work outside France. Carrier-Belleuse was asked to work in Belgium by the architect Suys, who was in charge of the works of the Bourse de Commerce of Brussels. Belleuse took Rodin, who accepted an exile which he expected to be short lived.

When he arrived in Brussels, Rodin was thirty years old, and an unknown world revealed itself to him;

he took advantage of what the circumstances could teach him and so began the most decisive phase of his evolution. He found in the baroque sculpture of Flanders the equivalent to Pierre Puget's works, which he admired. These influences, added to what Rodin knew of Michelangelo's sculpture, were of lasting import to the young artist.

In 1875, with little money, Rodin travelled to Rome on a trip essential to the conclusion of his years of apprenticeship. He stopped in Genoa, in Pisa and in Florence, where he stayed for five days. He studied the tombs of the Sacristy of San Lorenzo and commented later: "I believe that the great magician gave me some of his secrets." He returned to Rome to continue studying the works of Michelangelo, discovering at the same time the antiquities in the Vatican Museum. The importance of his trip can be seen in the works which Rodin executed upon his return. For the balustrade of the Garden of the Academies in Brussels he made a *Torso* symbolizing the Arts and directly inspired by the *Belvedere Torso*.

In 1876 he began the figure which, according to him, was to establish his reputation: *The Age of Bronze*. The statue was shown in January 1877 and was admired for a quality as precious as it was rare: the expression of life. Among the general praise one detected a malicious note: such approach to nature could only be the result of a casting taken from a living model. In order to obtain atonement and to dispel the infamous rumor, Rodin decided to submit the incriminated work to a Parisian jury. When it was shown in April 1877 at the Salon of the French Artists, the *Age of Bronze* caused the same scandal,

but the conflict with official art resulted in drawing attention to an artist who was almost unknown at the time.

The most productive part of Rodin's career begins in 1880 and lasts until 1900. The number and quality of the works which came out of his studio during this time lead us to believe that they were the result of his assiduous work and his experiences during the preceding twenty years.

Because Rodin received increasingly important commissions from the government of France, the official art world of the Academy recognized the sculptor. *The Gates of Hell* in 1888 was commissioned by the Government, the group of the *Burghers of Calais* in 1884 by the city of Calais, the monument of *Claude Lorrain* in 1889 by a Lorrain Committee for the Jardin de la Pépinière in Nancy, the two monuments of *Victor Hugo* in 1889 and 1891 by the city of Paris and the Government, the *Balzac* in 1892 by the Société des Gens de Lettres, and finally the monument of *President Sarmiento* in 1895 by the Argentinian Government for the city of Buenos Aires.

One must not forget the isolated groups, such as *The Kiss, Eternal Spring,* and *Eternal Idol.* The enormous amount of sculpture Rodin left to the world is matched in portent by the depth of feeling contained within each work. The secret of Rodin is summed up by a sentence with which he prefaced a catalog for an exhibition of his works: "The artist must return to the primitive text of God."

C Goldscheider

33. *The Kiss #9,* (*Le Baiser*), 1886. Bronze, 34 x 17 x 22 inches.

Biography

13

1840	November 12. Birth of Auguste Rodin in Paris.
1854	Entered School of Design and Mathematics, Paris.
1857	Rodin was refused admittance to the School of Fine Arts, Paris.
1862	Death of his sister, Marie. Entered the Convent of the Fathers of the Holy Sacrament.
1863	Returned to his family.
1864	Met Rose Beuret. Admitted to the workshop of Carrier-Belleuse. First offering to the Salon: *The Man with the Broken Nose.*
1866	Birth of his son, Auguste, who was to bear the family name of his mother.
1871	Left for Belgium with the artist, Carrier-Belleuse.
1872-74	Worked on the decoration of monuments in Brussels.
1875	Voyage to Italy.
1877	Exhibition of *The Age of Bronze* in Brussels.
1878	Returned to Paris permanently. Exhibition of *The Age of Bronze.*
1879	Worked in the manufacturing of Sèvres pieces.
1880	Commissioned to do *The Gates of Hell* and *Saint John the Baptist.*
1881	First attempted engraving. Completed sculptures: *Eve,* the busts of *Legros* and *J. P. Laurens.*
1883	Completed busts of *Dalou* and *Victor Hugo.*
1884	Commissioned to do *The Burghers of Calais.*
1886	Completed *The Kiss* and *Thought.*
1887	Completed *Monument of Bastien-Lepage* (Damvillers Cemetery).
1889	First commissioned to do *Monument of Victor Hugo. Monument of Claude Lorrain* (Garden of the Pépinière in Nancy). Completed *The Eternal Idol*

1890	Completed *Flying Figure. Iris, Messenger of the Gods.* Second commission to do *Monument of Victor Hugo.*
1892	Completed *Orpheus.*
1893	Commissioned to do statue of *Balzac* received from the Society of Men of Letters. Completed *Tower of Work.*
1895	Completed *Monument of President Sarmiento* for Buenos Aires.
1897	Completed *The Hand of God.*
1898	Exhibition of the statue of *Balzac* in the Salon. Project for the *Monument to Puvis De Chavannes.* Completed *Head of Baudelaire.*
1900	Exhibition held at the Alma Pavillion.
1901	Exhibition of sculpture at the Venice Biennale.
1902	Rodin Exhibition in Prague. First meeting with Rainer Marie-Rilke.
1904	Completed the sculpture, *France.*
1906	Completed *The Cambodians.* Portraits of *Bernard Shaw, Marcellin Berthelot, The Countess of Noailles.*
1908	Completed portrait of *Hanako.* Portrait of *Lacathedrale.* Moved to Hotel Biron.
1910	First publications of his thoughts on art: Article on *Venus De Milo* in "Art and Artists" in March and "L'Art" as told to Paul Gsell by Rodin.
1911	Completed bust of *Clemenceau.*
1914	Publication of "*Cathedrals of France*"—text reviewed by Charles Morice.
1915	Completed portrait of *Pope Benoit XV.*
1916	Rodin donated his works to the French nation.
1917	January 29. Marriage of Rodin to Rose Beuret.
1917	February 14. Death of Rose Beuret.
1917	November 17. Death of Rodin at Meudon.

List of Exhibitions

Early Works

15

1. *Man with the Broken Nose #8*, (*L'Homme au Nez Casse*), 1864. Bronze, 11 x 7 x 9 inches.

The first work presented by Rodin to be exhibited in the Salon des Artistes Français under the title: *Portrait of Monsieur B.* The model was a poor man, well known to the artists in the Saint-Marcel quarter, where Rodin worked at the time. In spite of its quality, the work was rejected by the Committee. The study was proof Rodin based his early style on classical models.

17

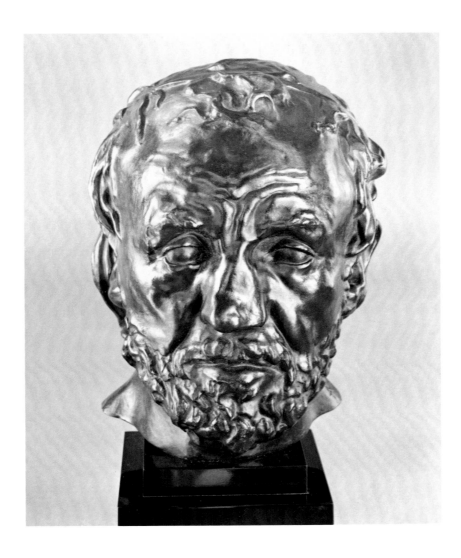

2. *Man with the Broken Nose, (L'Homme au Nez Casse)*, 1864. Plaster, $12\frac{1}{2}$ x $7\frac{1}{4}$ x 6 inches.

3. *Small Man with the Broken Nose #12, (Le Petit Homme au Nez Casse)*, 1882. Bronze, 5 x 3 x 4 inches.

Sketch modelled to fit in the narrow strip (of the upper part of the lintel) of the *Gates of Hell*, where Rodin had lined up small portraits of his contemporaries.

4. *Mignon #4*, (*Mignon*), 1870. Bronze, 16½ x 12½ x 10 inches.

Portrait of Rose Beuret, faithful companion to the sculptor and his model in the first years of their relationship. The plaster figures of her, nude or clothed, executed between 1865 and 1875 have not been preserved. Several portraits in marble (1890), in bronze, in terra cotta, even in ceramic (1911), show the transformation of a feminine face between youth and maturity. The shy character of Rose Beuret inspired Rodin's heroic bust of *Bellona* (*Bellone*) (1878).

5. *Head of a Young Boy #1*, (*Tête de Jeune Garçon*), about 1876. Bronze, 7 x 5½ x 6½ inches.

This portrait of a child is the only one known among Rodin's works. After the birth of his son in 1866, he made a number of sketches of young children and used them in works impregnated with tenderness and charm. Soon thereafter, he became disinterested in the transformation of the human being between infancy and adulthood except for some rare depictions of adolescent figures.

21

6. *The Age of Bronze* #10, *(Age d'Airain)*, 1876-1877. Bronze, 39 x 15½ x 13 inches.

This work, executed in Belgium after his return from Italy, was exhibited in January, 1877 in the Artistic Circle of Brussels under the title: *The Vanquished (Le Vaincu)*. It held the attention of the public—the model with his supple and firm body was the very essence of life without being realistic. This exceptional quality in his work was the basis of the accusation that he took molds from a living figure, a practice then current in the ateliers of sculptors.

Hoping to put an end to this suspicion, Rodin left Brussels for Paris in order to present his work to the Jury of the Salon des Artistes Français in April, 1878. Contrary to what he had expected, he found the opposition to his style of work stronger than ever in spite of the avant-garde critics, who were glad to support an artist who dared to reject academic tradition. In 1880, *The Age of Bronze* was again cast in bronze and exhibited in the same Salon. It was purchased by the State.

7. Saint John the Baptist #6, (Saint Jean-Baptiste),
1878-1880. Bronze, 32 x 13 x 21 inches.

The exhibition of this sculpture in 1880
followed that of *The Age of Bronze*. It con-
firmed the exceptional talent of a genius
whose early works were poorly understood.
The preacher is represented walking, his
mouth half open in the ecstasy of his preach-
ing. His attitude is that of *The Walking Man*
(*L'Homme Qui Marche*) with the same anom-
aly in the position of his legs, which are
spread apart.

The original *Saint John the Baptist* carried a
cross placed against his left shoulder which
explains the contraction of the arm and
hand on that side of his body.

23

24

The Burghers of Calais

25

In 1884, the city of Calais decided to again take up an old project of erecting a monument in remembrance of the heroism of six burghers who had sacrificed their lives in order to save the city which was beseiged by the King of England in 1347. A journalist of the time, Jean Froissart, related the facts in "Les Grandes Chroniques de France" written shortly afterwards. The six heroes, he wrote, were ordered to present themselves, with heads uncovered, barefoot, and with a cord around their necks, before the King to give him the keys to the city.

Rodin studied the text thoroughly in order to draw up a first sketch, which was approved by the Calais municipality on January 23, 1885. The production of this work started off quite actively; three figures were exhibited in May, 1886, and the three others were sufficiently far along to forecast the bronze fountain would be finished by autumn. Then suddenly everything stopped because of a financial disaster in the city. Negotiations were resumed in 1888 but Rodin, who was absorbed by other works and his health suffering from overwork, demanded new delays and the monuments were not inaugurated until June 3, 1895.

All the preparatory sketches have been conserved.

26

8. *Study for Eustache de Saint-Pierre #4, (Étude pour Eustache de Sainte-Pierre)*, 1887. Bronze, $38\frac{1}{2}$ x $12\frac{1}{2}$ x 15 inches.

He is the most popular person in the group; he is also the oldest. Two studies of nudes with different heads reveal the hardship of the march and the difficulty of self-denial. In the final monument, Eustache de Saint-Pierre is immobile in the middle of his companions, his head on his chest, his arms hanging loosely, vividly expressing the resolution of his departure, without hope of return.

27

9. *Andrieu d'Andres #11, (Andrieu d'Andres)*.
Bronze, 18½ x 7¾ x 8½ inches.

Responding to the desires of several admirers and collectors, Rodin consented to make small casts of five figures in the group; the first was executed in 1899.

29

10. *Jean d'Aire* (*Jean d'Aire*), 1904. Ceramic, 18 x 20½ x 10¼ inches.

"A very solid bourgeois, a man of affairs who had two beautiful girls." It is in these terms that he is presented in the recitation of Froissart. It is he who fiercely holds the key to the city in his powerful hands, contracted with the enormous effort.

Rodin had worked from 1879 to 1882 for the manufacturer of Sèvres porcelain. He had an interest in ceramics and entrusted to Jeanneney the execution of some pieces much sought after today.

11. *Hand of a Burgher of Calais #4*, (*Main d'un Bourgeois de Calais*). Bronze, 11 x 7½ x 6 inches.

For Rodin, hands were as expressive as faces, and he took great care in their execution. Those of the Burghers of Calais were studied particularly and emphasized the intensity of the gesture, revealing the personality of each man. This is the left hand of Pierre de Wiessant.

32

33 In 1880, Rodin received from the National Government the commission for a monumental door destined for the Musée des Arts Décoratifs, which was to be constructed on the left bank of the Seine, facing the Tuilleries garden. The initial project is known by several designs and recalls the *Gates of Paradise* by Ghiberti on the Baptistry in Florence, but the regularity and order in the first sketches were soon followed by chaos. An unfinished three-dimensional transposition of a vast fresco recalls the acute representations of Michelangelo, Signorelli, and Rubens. The monumental work offered a synthesis of Rodin's ideas, of his torment and of his dreams. To the grandeur of "The Divine Comedy"—which had long been familiar to Rodin—the sculptor added the despair inherent in Baudelaire's writing. *Hell (L'Enfer)* and *The Flowers of Evil (Les Fleurs du Mal)* unite to express the anguish of a world without hope.

The Gates of Hell contain the main concerns of Rodin's sculptural ambition. He drew from his inexhaustible reserve of forms; he elaborated and transformed the principal themes in adapting them to new ends.

In the exhibition at the Pavillon of Alma in 1900, the base alone, without the figures, was presented to the public. The door did not take its present form until July, 1917. Four studies in bronze were completed and are to be found at the Musée Rodin in Paris, the Rodin Museum in Philadelphia, the Kunsthaus in Zürich, and the Museum of Occidental Art in Tokyo.

The Gates of Hell

34

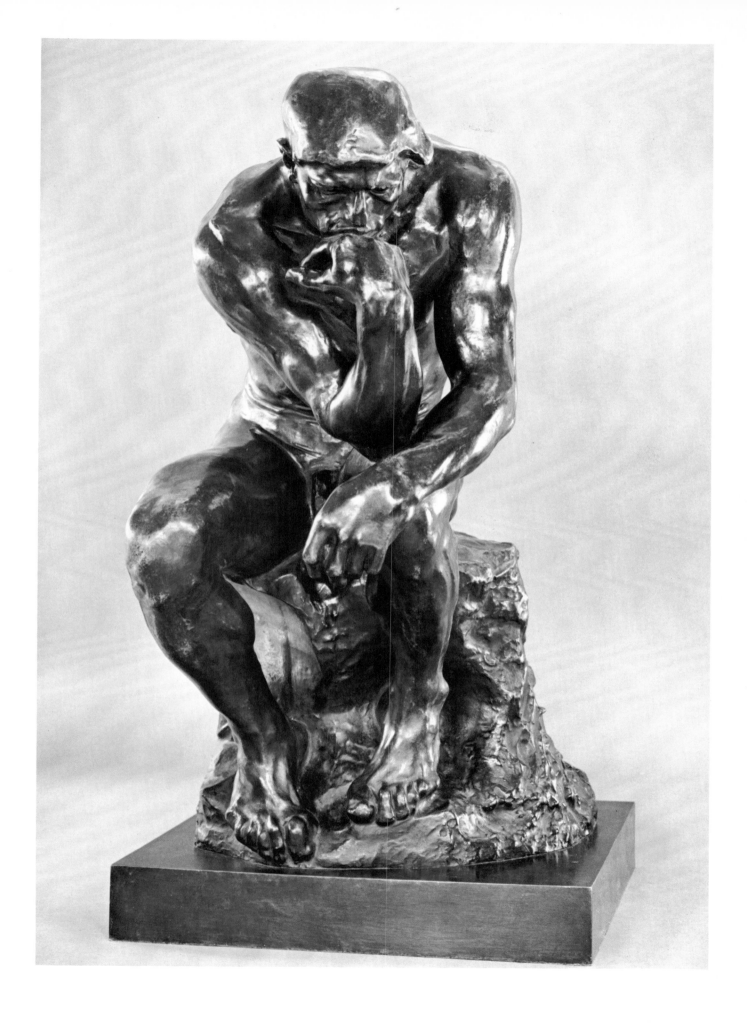

Previous Page: 12. *The Thinker #9, (Le Penseur)*, 1880. Bronze, 28 x 14 x 23 inches.

This figure is detached in a jutting position in the center of the lintel; an axial figure, it dominates the chaotic vision of Hell, a symbol of the poet in a Dantesque fashion. An enlarged version was placed in front of the Pantheon in Paris in 1906. Another study was placed, according to the will of Rodin, on his tomb in the garden of the Villa des Brillants in Meudon.

13. *Eve #12, (Eve)*, 1881. Bronze, 28 x 10 x 10½ inches.

A reduced figure of the statue conceived to be placed on one of the sides of the *Gates of Hell,* Adam was placed on the other side.

Rodin chose to represent the confusion which followed the original sin, the sense of guilt and disgrace, even while the robust fullness of the forms evoke the fecundity of the Mother of Humanity.

14. *The Crouching Woman #4, (La Femme Accroupie)*, 1882. Bronze, 37½ x 25 x 22 inches.

An enlargement of a figure placed in the lintel of the *Gates of Hell.* The head, alone, is known as *Lust (Luxure).* In the Boston Museum a variation exists in marble which carries a block on its shoulder and is thus called by another name, *Caryatid with a Stone (Cariatide à la Pierre).*

36

15. *I am Beautiful...*, (*Je Suis Belle...*), 1882. Plaster, 28 x 11½ x 12½ inches.

This group, originally titled *The Abductor* (*l'Enlèvement*), is composed of two figures separated in the *Gates of Hell*: *The Crouching Woman* and *The Fallen Man* (*L'Homme Qui Tombe*), both placed in the summit of the door on the left.

The first words of a poem by Baudelaire engraved on the base read:

> I am beautiful, O Mortals, live a
>   dream of stone
> And my breast on which each has been
>   murdered one by one
> Is there to inspire the poet with love
> Eternal and silent as matter

In 1888, Rodin illustrated a copy of *The Flowers of Evil* for the editor, Gallimard. (This copy is today part of the collection of the Musée Rodin.)

16. *Torso of a Man #4*, (*Torse d'Homme*). Bronze, 10¼ x 7¼ x 3½ inches.

Study of a male for the *Gates of Hell*.

17. *Kneeling Faunesse #11, (Faunesse à Genoux)*, 1884. Bronze, 21¼ x 9 x 11½ inches.

A figure placed in the lintel of the *Gates of Hell*. The same feminine type, supple and muscular, is used by Rodin for the *Standing Faunesse (Faunesse Debout)*, and several figures of the damned. The face is void of human expression. The face with wrinkled cheeks and protruding jaw in its animal aggressiveness contrasts with the harmonious beauty of the body.

The same faunesse has become the principal person in the group *Orpheus and the Maenads (Orphée et Les Ménades)*.

18. *She Who Was the Helmet-Maker's Beautiful Wife #5, (Celle Qui Fut la Belle Heaulmiere)*, 1884. Bronze, 19¾ x 12⅛ x 9 inches.

Treated in shallow relief, this image of an old woman appears on one of the pilasters of the *Gates of Hell*. This shriveled feminine body recalls the *Magdeline* of Donatello in the Baptistry in Florence, but the latter shows a face illuminated by faith while the sinner of Rodin cries for lost beauty.

Carrying the figure of an adolescent on her knees, this work gave birth to a group entitled *Triumphant Youth (La Jeunesse Triomphante)*. At the exhibition in 1899 which combined the works of Claude Monet and Rodin, the sculptor presented a group composed of two studies of this same figure under the name *The Broken Sources (Sources Taries)*.

Back view: 18. *She Who Was the Helmet-Maker's Beautiful Wife #5, (Celle Qui Fut la Belle Heaulmiere)*, 1884. Bronze, 19¾ x 12⅛ x 9 inches.

19. *The Earth #8, (La Terre)*, 1884-1900. Bronze, 8 x 18½ x 6½ inches.

The transformation of a figure in high relief presented on the door of the *Gates of Hell*, back view, standing up, legs crossed. In a bad firing of the clay, the legs were broken; Rodin, who kept even the defective works, later used it, thus creating an image which was not originally intended but which was the result of an accident.

20. *Study of a Woman Damned #10,*
(Étude pour une Damnée), 1885. Bronze,
8 x 15½ x 10¼ inches.

A figure placed in the right half of the lintel
of the *Gates of Hell,* lying at the feet of the
Standing Faunesse.

21. *Women Damned*, *(Femmes Damnées)*, 1885. Plaster, 8 x 10¾ x 5 inches.

A group composed of two figures each located on the *Gates of Hell*. The restless anatomy of the faunesses is apparent. This plaster was part of the collection of Anthony Roux.

Following page: 22. *The Martyr #5*, *(La Martyre)*, 1885. Bronze, 4½ x 24 x 17 inches.

A figure conceived for the *Gates of Hell* where it was placed in the lintel. It is one of Rodin's most original creations and he used it several times. Enlarged and isolated, she is full of voluptuous and passionate beauty.

She represents *Lust* in the couple entitled *Avarice and Lust* (*L'Avarice et la Luxure*). She is the principal figure in a decorative ensemble commissioned by the Baron Vitta for the vestibule of his Villa d'Evion la Sapinière. Rodin adapted it in high relief for the funerary monument of the poet Sourisseau in 1909 in the cemetery in Saint-Acheul (Amiens), giving her wings and calling it *The Broken Lily* (*Le Lys Brisé*).

45

23. *Danaïde #4*, (*La Danaïde*), 1885. Bronze, 12¾ x 28¼ x 22½ inches.

First destined for the *Gates of Hell*, this work was removed in order to be presented alone on a rock. The nude is one of the most beautiful done by the artist in his maturity.

24. *Glaucus*, (*Glaucus*), 1886-1887. Plaster, 8 x 6¾ x 5½ inches.

A group partially formed by a figure of an old man appearing on the *Gates of Hell*. The siren crouched against him is the transformation of a small woman damned, being carried off in a whirlwind on one of the doors.

This piece was in the collection of Anthony Roux.

25. *The Three Sirens #5, (Les Trois Sirènes),*
1887. Bronze, 18 x 16 x 12 inches.

This group, one of the smallest in size, rises
from a rock base on the left side of the
Gates of Hell. Rodin enlarged it while giving
more freedom to each of the figures for the
second monument of Victor Hugo. At
the foot of the rock dominated by the poet,
they symbolize the voices of the sea.

26. *The Prodigal Son #8, (L'Enfant Prodigue),*
1888. Bronze, 55 x 42½ x 28 inches.

This single figure is enlarged into a person-
age who appears in different aspects in the
Gates of Hell; the *Despairing Adolescent*
(*L'Adolescent Désespéré*), the *Kneeling Man*
(*L'Homme à Genoux*) with his arms folded
behind his head. He is essentially the figure
in the group, *Fleeting Love (Fugit Amor),*
where two people pursue an impossible em-
brace, such as in *Paolo and Francesca.*

The tension in the body, shaped like an arc,
is in opposition to the figures lying pros-
trate on top of each other. Rodin vascil-
lates between the two tendencies: the
depiction of the effort of man towards freedom (*Orpheus, The Centauresse, Invocation*) or
the depiction of a timeless fatalism (*The
Crouching Woman, Danaïde, Caryatid*).

27. *Polypheme #9*, (*Polypheme*), 1888. Bronze, 10 x 5 x 6½ inches.

A figure located on the right side of the *Gates of Hell*. In the original, the cyclops, amorous of Galatea, surprises her in the arms of the young shepherd, Acis, and is about to crush them with a rock. Rodin decided not to show the couple but kept the posture of the giant leaning over the abyss.

28. *Large Clenched Left Hand #3*, (*Grande Main Crispée Gauche*), 1888. Bronze, 18¾ x 10¾ x 6 inches.

Enlargement of a hand of one of the damned, being dragged towards the abyss.

29. *Study for Despair*, (*Étude pour le Désespoir*),
1890. Plaster, 11 x 5¾ x 6¾ inches.

54

30. *Despair #12*, (*Le Désespoir*), 1890.
Bronze, $13\frac{1}{2}$ x $10\frac{1}{2}$ x 12 inches.

A figure placed in the right side of the
Gates of Hell. The model who posed for this
posed for *Danaïde*.

55

56

Assortment of Groups and Single Figures

58

31. *Eternal Spring #6*, (*L'Eternel Printemps*), 1884. Bronze, 25½ x 28¼ x 16 inches.

The representation of the couple occupied an important place in the work of Rodin, because the piece represented a liberation from academic tradition.

Eternal Spring is the exaltation of youth. The young man with his back showing the trace of wings identifies him as Eros. The girl kneeling at his feet can be found in *Torso of Adèle* in the *Gates of Hell*, in *Illusions Received on Earth* (*Illusions Reçues par la Terre*), and in *The Fallen Angel* (*Chute d'un Ange*).

There are several marbles of the same subject, which, during Rodin's lifetime, received acclaim equal to *The Kiss*.

32. *Iris Surprising a Nymph, (Iris Éveillant une Nymphe)*, 1885. Plaster, 13¾ x 10¾ x 8½ inches.

An elegant group once in the collection of Anthony Roux. It is sometimes called *Venus and Love*.

33. *The Kiss, (Le Baiser)*, 1886. Plaster, 34 x 20½ x 21 inches.

It is considered the most classical work of Rodin in spite of the novelty of the subject, inspired by the 5th Canto of Hell which evokes the love of Paolo Malatesta and Francesca da Rimini. Stripped of all reality which would stand in the way of the grandeur of the subject, it is treated with devotion, without mannerisms or false sentimentality. The work brought success to Rodin during his lifetime. As

with *Eternal Spring*, the artist authorized the Barbedienne Foundry to reproduce the study in four different sizes.

There are three groups in marble of monumental size at the Musée Rodin in Paris, Glyptothèque Ny Carlsberg in Copenhagen, and the Tate Gallery in London.

34. *Eternal Idol #9*, (*L'Eternelle Idole*), 1889. Bronze, 11¾ x 10 x 5 inches.

Grasping the theme of the couple, Rodin searched for diversity in it; he expressed in several works the silent adoration of man for woman and his submission before love. In this regard, *Man and His Thoughts* (*L'Homme et sa Pensée*), *Pygmalion and Galatea* (*Pygmalion et Galatée*) preceded *Eternal Idol*. The group here attained a degree of perfection rarely equalled. It is necessary to consider it from all angles to establish the unimpeachable position of the two people. Whatever angle from which it is viewed, there is always a new aspect to be seen. On an emotional level, the duality of the sexes is apparent in the indifference of the woman to the homage the man is rendering to her beauty.

35. *Toilet of Venus #4*, (*La Toilette de Venus*), 1886. Bronze, 18 x 9½ x 8 inches.

The attitude of this figure recalls that of the *Kneeling Faunesse* but the body is more supple, the play of the muscles more relaxed. There are several studies in marble of the same female figure, the presentation offering some variety. Rodin made a *Siren* out of her by transforming the legs into a fishtail.

36. *The Bather, (Baigneuse)*, 1888. Plaster, 14½ x 7 x 8¼ inches.

Rodin made several studies of the female body. He loved the theme of the bather coming out of the waves. Several figures were inspired by the same model. Certain watercolors denote the same studies— the suppleness of a body in motion as one would see it in water.

The work was part of the collection of Anthony Roux.

37. *Venus #12, (Venus)*, 1888. Bronze, 20 x 2¾ x 5¼ inches.

This study of a nude was copied for Pierre Louy's theatrical production "Aphrodite". The figure was slightly modified with the arms folded behind the head.

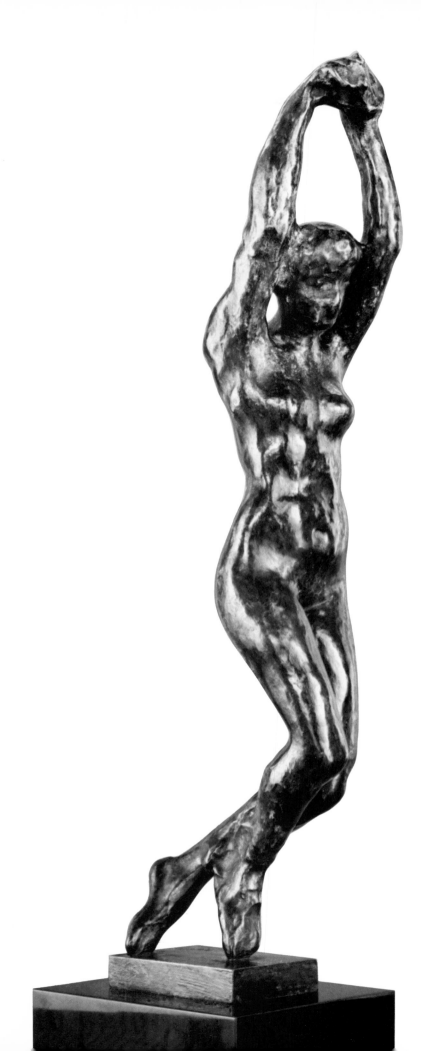

38. *Iris, Messenger of the Gods #12,*
(*Iris, Messagère des Dieux*), 1890. Bronze,
18 x 18¼ x 7¼ inches.

The boldness of this work is related to the
studies of movements of models who
were celebrated dancers in Montmarte.
The movements were broken down
into the difficult exercises required for the
French Cancan and Chahut.

39. *Flying Figure #1, (Figure Volante)*, 1890.
Bronze, 17 x 29 x 12½ inches.

This sculpture has the same origins as
the preceding one. In 1890 Rodin began his
collection of antique sculpture. He acquired pieces of broken sculptures and little
by little his taste led him to judge these
works as fragments with their own aesthetic.

In a letter to his wife, Rainier Marie-Rilke,
who came to Rodin in 1902 to write
a monograph on his works, describes the
workshop as follows:

> "Nothing but pieces, hardly anything
> whole; here a simple piece of arm, there
> a part of a leg, to one side the torso of a
> body; the torso of a statue with the
> head of another model and the arm of a
> third statue glued to it. Like a mad
> tempest, an unprecedented cataclysm
> had swept over his work."

40. *Study of a Woman's Torso #4*, (*Étude de Femme à Mi-Corps*), 1910. Bronze, 29 x 18 x 25 inches.

The movement of the torso is reminiscent of *The Martyr*, but grief here is transformed into juvenile charm.

41. *Pas-de-Deux "G" #6*, (*Pas-de-Deux "G"*), 1910-1913. Bronze, 13½ x 7 x 6¾ inches.

Rodin has rarely represented the human being at rest. To him all movement meant transformation, and he was a passionate observer of the dance. He was not touched, as Degas was, by classical dance. An enemy by instinct of all conventions, he turned to the boldest forms of choreography. He received in his workshop the eccentric dancers of Montmartre from Toulouse-Lautrec. The innovations of the American dancer Loïe Fuller who made her debut in Paris in

1892 seduced him. A few years later, Isadora Duncan revealed to him the soul of ancient dances. In 1896 and in 1906 he learned the mystery of religious dances of the Orient from Javanese and Cambodian dancers. Lastly, the Russian Ballet brought him new inspiration.

These observations are illustrated in numerous drawings and watercolors in which the figures of dancers are caught in the spirit of improvisation.

68

42. *The Cry #12, (Le Cri)*, 1898. Bronze, 10½ x 12½ x 8 inches.

This is an intensely painful and anguished figure and cannot be compared to any known work.

The idea is repeated in *The Tempest (La Tempête)* in a composition which has less pathos.

43. *The Man with One Ear #12, (L'Homme à une Oreille)*. Bronze, 5 x 3¼ x 5 inches.

It is known that Rodin after visiting Parisian hospitals returned home to model from memory the physical anomalies which he had observed. Many heads, often in terra cotta, bear testimony to these visits.

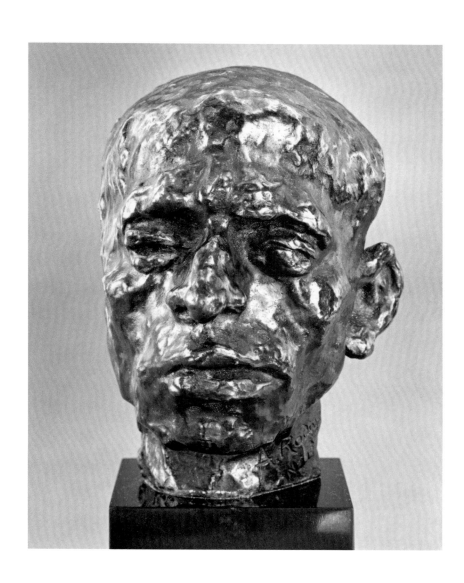

44. *Head of a Blind Slave #11, (Tête d' Esclave Aveugle)*. Bronze, 5½ x 3½ x 5¼ inches.

The origins of the sad face are identical to the preceding work. These studies of physical pain had no determined purpose.

45. *Head of a Man No.228 #8, (Tête d'Homme No.228).* Bronze, 4½ x 4¼ x 3½ inches.

This head was used for one of the first study models of *The Burghers of Calais.*

73

46. *Henri Becque #4*, (*Henri Becque*), 1883. Bronze, 6 x 3¼ x 2¾ inches.

Rodin has left the most vivid image of the society of his times in a series of portraits, the oldest of which dates back to 1862. Writers, such as Henri Becque, author of "Crows" and "The Parisian", art critics, painters and sculptors, politicians, the bourgeois and international nobility bear testimony to his reputation.

47. *Head of Camille Claudel #1*, (*Tête de Camille Claudel*), 1884. Bronze, 11 x 8 x 7 inches.

Pupil and collaborator of Rodin, Camille Claudel left a work which reveals original and personal talent. She held a great place in the emotional life of the sculptor who was at once seduced by her beauty and intelligence. She was associated with his life and his work during his most fruitful years, from *The Gates of Hell* to *Balzac*.

Rodin made many portraits of her under other titles, such as *Farewell* (*Adieu*), *The Aurora* (*L'Aurore*), *Saint George* (*Sainte-Georges*), *The Convalescent* (*La Convalescente*), *Thought* (*La Pensée*) and *France*.

48. *Camille Claudel with a Bonnet #4,*
(Camille Claudel au Bonnet), 1886. Bronze,
10 x 5½ x 6 inches.

This portrait is a study for *Thought,* the head
of a woman emerging from a block of
marble.

49. *France #4, (La France)*, 1904. Bronze,
20 x 18 x 12½ inches.

A work inspired by the face of Camille
Claudel. This was placed in the monument
inaugurated in 1912 on the shores of Lake
Champlain. The bust became the symbolic
image of France and does homage to the
Frenchman who discovered the lake which
today bears his name.

50. *Mask of Iris #12, (Masque d'Iris)*, 1890.
Bronze, 4 x 3 x 3 inches.
Rodin made many enlargements of this
mask which he isolated from the *Gates of
Hell*.

51. *Head of Iris #4, (Tête d'Iris)*, 1890.
Bronze, 24 x 13 x 13 inches.

A fragment of a colossal statue which was
never executed, it is an enlargement of the
small *Mask of Iris*.

50. *Mask of Iris #12, (Masque d'Iris)*, 1890.
Bronze, 4 x 3 x 3 inches.
Rodin made many enlargements of this
mask which he isolated from the *Gates of
Hell*.

51. *Head of Iris #4, (Tête d'Iris)*, 1890.
Bronze, 24 x 13 x 13 inches.

A fragment of a colossal statue which was
never executed, it is an enlargement of the
small *Mask of Iris*.

52. *Hanako #7, (Hanako)*, 1908. Bronze, 12 x 8 x 6 inches.

Portrait of a Japanese dancer. Loïe Fuller introduced her to Rodin when he singled her out from Miss Fuller's ballet troupe. He made many portraits of her towards the end of his career, which are among his best pieces.

53. *Head of the Dancer Nijinsky #5, (Tête du Danseur Nijinsky)*, 1912. Bronze, 2½ x 1¼ x 1½ inches.

On the day after the first presentation of the "Afternoon of a Faun" on May 29, 1912, when the Russian dancer received triumphal acclaim both as an actor and as a director, he visited Rodin at his studio. Rodin had expressed his enthusiasm in a note to the press by praising a form of dance which he particularly admired.

The sitting lasted only the one day but was sufficient for Rodin to make rapid designs of the dancer's movements and model a small figure which would fix a position. The small head was doubtless made from memory. Thanks to Cocteau's drawings, it could be identified.

54. *Benedict XV #7*, *(Benoît XV)*, 1915.
Bronze, 10 x 7 x 9½ inches.

At the time of his last trip to Rome lasting
from April 8 into the first days of May,
Rodin obtained three sittings from the
Sovereign Pontiff for this portrait, one of
Rodin's last works.

55. *Victor Hugo #5*, *(Victor Hugo)*, 1897.
Bronze, 28 x 18¾ x 18¾ inches.

In 1883 Rodin had made the bust of Victor
Hugo. He struck up a friendship with the
poet but the latter never posed for him.

When Rodin received the commission of a
monument for the cemetery, he made rough
sketches of the portrait for different
maquettes.

He knew how to transpose the initial portrait by enlarging it and this bust corresponds to the likeness of the poet in the
finished monument.

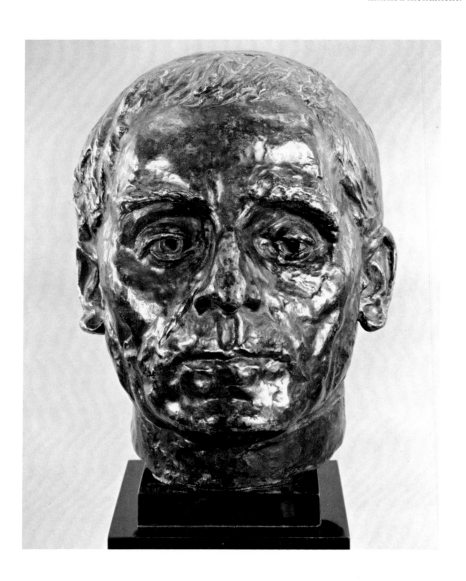

84

56. *Study of Nude for Balzac A #11, (Étude de Nu pour Balzac A)*, 1892-1897. Bronze, 14¼ x 10¼ x 6¾ inches.

Rodin never knew Balzac. In order to secure his image, he availed himself of the novelist's portraits and his literary works.

57. *Study of Nude for Balzac B #12, (Étude de Nu Pour Balzac B)*. Bronze, 11½ x 3½ x 4 inches.

A small statue which evokes the athletic body of *Study of Nude for Balzac F*.

58. *Study for Balzac C #6, (Étude pour Balzac C)*, 1893. Bronze, 30 x 12½ x 15 inches.

Rodin noted in the journal of Goncourt (1855) this portrait:

"Gavarni still tells us that physically Balzac from the back of the head to the heels formed a straight line with only one flabby spot. As for the front of the novelist, it was a veritable Ace of Spades."

58. bis. *Study for Balzac C #4, (Étude pour Balzac C)*, 1893. Bronze, 50¼ x 20½ x 24¾ inches.

A larger study of the preceding sculpture, donated to the Los Angeles County Museum of Art by Mr. B. Gerald Cantor.

59. *Study of Nude for Balzac F #1, "Athlete," (Étude de Nu pour Balzac F, "Athlete.")* Bronze, 38 x 16 x 14 inches.

A nude athlete which Rodin made different attempts to clothe. It corresponds to the portrait made by Balzac's contemporaries who called him the "courageous athlete."

60. *Monumental Head of Balzac* (*Tête Monumentale de Balzac*), 1897-1904. Ceramic, 18½ x 16 x 12 inches.

After being inspired by portraits of the novelist made available to him by a friend who had secured them from Count Lovenjoul, Rodin produced a symbolic image of the author of "Comédie Humaine". In Chapter V in the work of Lamartine, "Balzac and His Works" (1866), Rodin had written in the margin of his edition: "Portrait of B" and then underlined with two lines the last sentence which begins: "he was big, heavy—square at the bottom and at the shoulders." Such was the man in his robust frame but on looking at the face, one did not see the frame. The face seemed to talk and one could not turn away from it; it charmed and fascinated one completely.

Hands

94

61. *The Hand of God #9, (La Main de Dieu)*,
1897. Bronze, 13 x 13 x 11 inches.

In the study for the sculpture in marble,
the sculptor has placed in the enlarged right
hand of a Burgher of Calais (Pierre de
Wiessant) a couple rising from the material.
The creation of the couple has taken
on another form in terra cotta where the
creator shelters the two figures of the
Eternal Idol.

61. *The Hand of God #9, (La Main de Dieu)*, 1897. Bronze, 13 x 13 x 11 inches.

62. *Large Hand of a Pianist #1, (Grande Main de Pianiste)*. Bronze, $7\frac{1}{2}$ x $10\frac{1}{4}$ x 5 inches.

Rodin loved music. Among his friends, the musicians revealed to him the universal grandeur of Beethoven and of Mozart. The harpsichordist, Wanda Landowska, gave concerts at Meudon. Rodin followed the movement of her hands on the keys. His observations have been left in his studies, done with great precision.

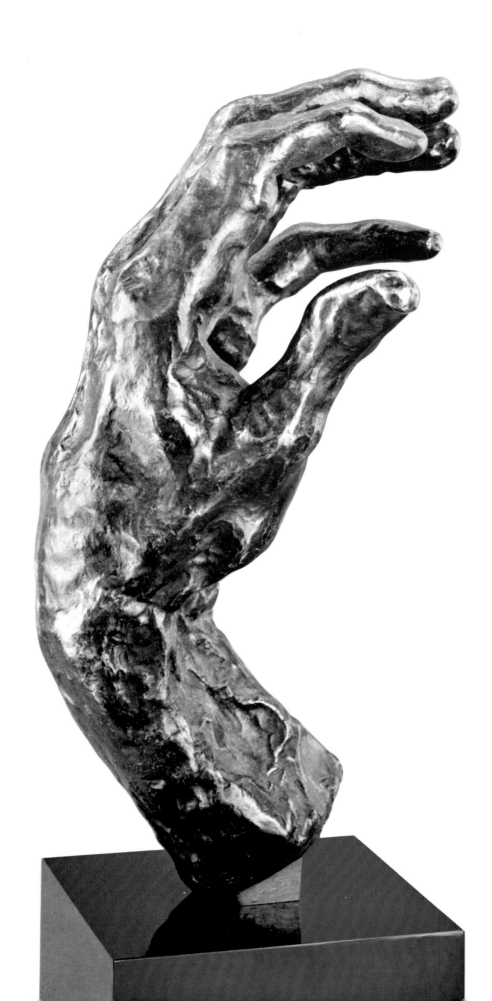

63. *Large Left Hand #4, (Grande Main Gauche).* Bronze, 13 x 6½ x 7 inches.

64. *Hand No. 35 #6, (Main No. 35).* Bronze, 3⅛ x 6 x 2¼ inches.

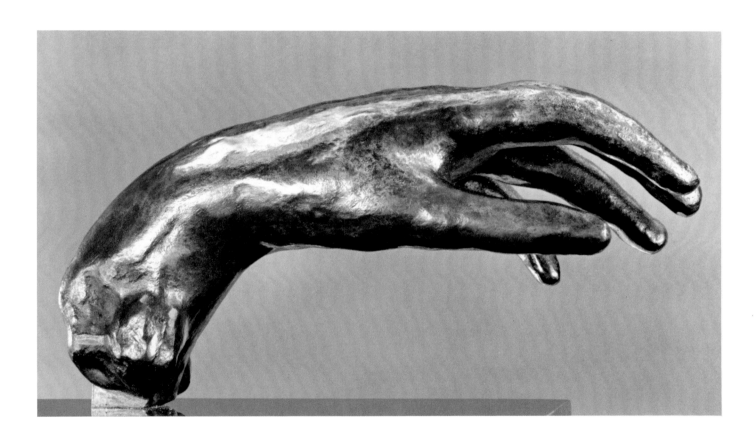

65. *Hand No. 21 #5, (Main No. 21).* Bronze, 2¾ x 1¼ x ¾ inches.

66. *Hand No. 33 #1, (Main No. 33).* Bronze, 4¾ x 2⅞ x 6 inches.

67. *Hand No. 37 #4, (Main No. 37).* Bronze, $4\frac{7}{8}$ x 3 x $1\frac{7}{8}$ inches.

68. *Hand of Rodin with Torso #3, (Main de Rodin avec Torse),* 1917. Bronze, 7 x 9 x $5\frac{1}{2}$ inches.

The mold for Rodin's hand was made three weeks before his death. It has a small twist in it which he modelled.

Selective Bibliography

Compiled by *Ellen Landis*

ALLEY, RONALD. *Tate Gallery Catalogs: Foreign Paintings, Drawings, and Sculpture.* London, Shenval Press, 1959. Pp. 205-227.

BARTLETT, TRUMAN H. "Auguste Rodin, Sculptor", *American Architect and Building News.* XXV, Nos. 682-703. January-June, 1889. Serialized interview in ten installments.

BOURDELLE, ANTOINE. *La Sculpture et Rodin* . . . Paris, Emile-Paul, 1937.

BRANCUSI, CONSTANTIN. "Hommage à Rodin". *Quatrième Salon de la Jeune Sculpture.* Exhibition Catalog. Paris, Gizard, 1952.

BRECK, JOSEPH. "The Collection of Sculptures by Auguste Rodin in The Metropolitan Museum of Art", *Metropolitan Museum of Art Bulletin*, May, 1912, Supplement; reissued August, 1913.

Camera Work. Nos. 34 and 35, April-July, 1911. Including photographs of Rodin and his work by Edward Steichen and special articles by Benjamin de Casseres and Agnes Ernst Meyer.

DE CASO, JACQUES. "Rodin and the Cult of Balzac". *The Burlington Magazine.* June, 1964. Pp. 279-284.

DE CASO, JACQUES. "Balzac and Rodin in Rhode Island". *Bulletin of Rhode Island School of Design.* Vol. 52, No. 4.

CHAMPIGNEULLE, BERNARD. *Rodin.* New York, Abrams, 1967.

CLADEL, JUDITH. "Rodin", in Benezit, E., *Dictionnaire des peintres, sculpteurs, dessinateurs et graveurs,* New Edition. Paris, Grund, 1954, VII, Pp. 299-303.

CLADEL, JUDITH. *Rodin, sa vie glorieuse, sa vie inconnue.* Paris, Gallimard, 1936. Definitive edition: Paris, Grasset, 1950. English translation by James Whitall, New York, Harcourt, Brace, 1937.

CLARIS, EDMOND. *De l'Impressionisme en sculpture.* Paris, La Nouvelle Revue, 1902.

COGNIAT, RAYMOND. "Rodin". In Maillard, Robert, *Dictionary of Modern Sculpture.* New York, Tudor, (1960). Pp. 254-258.

DELTEIL, LOYS. *Rude, Barye, Carpeaux, Rodin, Le Peintre-graveur illustre, XIXe et XXe siècles.* Vol. 6. Paris, Chez l'auteur, 1910.

DESCHARNES, ROBERT AND CHABRUN, JEAN FRANCAIS. *Auguste Rodin.* Lausanne, Inedita, 1967.

DIRCKS, RUDOLF, *Auguste Rodin.* London, Siegle, Hill, 1909.

Auguste Rodin, Readings on His Life and Work. Edited and with an introduction by Albert Elsen. New Jersey, Prentice-Hall, 1965.

ELSEN, ALBERT E. "The Genesis of Rodin's Gates of Hell", *Magazine of Art,* XLV, March, 1952. Pp. 100-119.

ELSEN, ALBERT E. "The Humanism of Rodin and Lipchitz", *College Art Journal,* XLVII, Spring, 1958. Pp. 247-265.

ELSEN, ALBERT E. *Rodin.* New York, Doubleday, 1963.

ELSEN, ALBERT E. *Rodin's Gates of Hell.* Minneapolis, University of Minnesota, 1960.

FRISCH, VICTOR AND SHIPLEY, JOSEPH T. *Auguste Rodin, A Biography.* New York, Stokes, 1939.

GEISSBUHLER, ELIZABETH CHASE. *Rodin: Later Drawings* with Interpretations by Antoine Bourdelle. Boston, Beacon Press, 1963.

Auguste Rodin Zeichnungen. Edited by C. Goldscheider, with an introduction by Rainier Marie-Rilke. Munich, R. Piper & Coverlag, 1962.

JIANOU, IONEL AND GOLDSCHEIDER, CÉCILE. *Rodin.* Paris, Arted, Editions d'Art, 1967.

KAHN, GUSTAVE. *Auguste Rodin.* L'Art et le beau. Paris, 1906.

LAWTON, FREDERICK. *The Life and Work of Auguste Rodin.* New York, Scribners, 1907.

Rodin Drawings. Edited by Stephen Longstreet. Alhambra, California, Borden Press.

LUDOVICI, ANTHONY M. *Personal Reminiscences of Auguste Rodin.* Philadelphia, Lippincott, 1926.

MAILLARD, LEON. *Auguste Rodin, statuaire.* Paris, H. Floury, 1899.

MARTINIE, A. HENRI. *Auguste Rodin, 1840-1917.* Paris, Braun & Cie.

MARTINIE, A. HENRI. *Rodin.* Paris, Les Editions Braun & Cie, 1947.

NATHANSON, THADÉE. "Auguste Rodin" *Arts de France,* VII, 1946. Pp. 24-34.

RIPLEY, ELIZABETH. *Rodin, A Biography.* New York, Lippincott, 1966.

Rodin, The Man and His Art, with leaves from his Notebook. Compiled by Judith Cladel. English Translation by S. K. Starr. New York, Century Co., 1918.

Rodin. Introduction by Sommerville Story. London, Phaidon, 1961.

"Rodin's Balzac in the Museum of Modern Art, New York" *Art Quarterly,* XVIII, No. 4, 1955. Pp. 419-421.

RODIN, AUGUSTE. *A la Venus de Milo.* Paris, Le Jeune Parque, 1945. Reprinted from *L'Art et les Artistes,* March, 1910.

RODIN, AUGUSTE. *Les Cathedrales de France.* Introduction by Charles Morice. Paris, Colin, 1914. New Edition: English translation by E. C. Geissbuhler. Boston, Beacon Press, 1965.

SUTTON, DENYS. *Rodin.* Penguin Series of Sculptors, edited by John Russell. London, Penguin, 1963.

107 SUTTON, DENYS. *Triumphant Satyr: The World of Auguste Rodin*. New York, Hawthorn, 1966.

TIREL, MARCELLE. *Rodin Intime*. Preface by Judith Cladel. Paris, Edition du Monde Nouveau, 1923.

TYLER, PARKER. "Rodin and Freud: Masters of Ambivalence," *Art News*, LIV, March, 1955. Pp. 38-41, 63-64.

BEIRUT, LEBANON. Musée Nicolas Sursock. *Auguste Rodin*. Exhibition Catalog. April 13-June 15, 1964.

CALAIS, MUSÉE DU CALAIS, *Exposition Rodin, Commemoration du Cinquantenaire de la Mort d'Artiste*. Exhibition Catalog. July 1-August 30, 1967.

LONDON, ARTS COUNCIL OF GREAT BRITAIN. *Rodin*. Exhibition Catalog. 1966-1967.

NEW YORK, CHARLES E. SLATKIN GALLERIES. *Rodin, Sculptures and Drawings*. Exhibition Catalog, 1963.

PARIS, MUSÉE DU LOUVRE. *Rodin inconnu*. Exhibition Catalog. December, 1962-January, 1963.

PARIS, MUSÉE RODIN. *Balzac et Rodin*. Exhibition Catalog. 1950.

PRAGUE, MUSEUM. *Exposition Rodin*. Exhibition Catalog. July 13-September 15, 1967.

ROME, VILLA MEDICI, ACCADEMIA DI FRANCIA. *Mostra di Auguste Rodin*. Exhibition Catalog. May 26-June 30, 1967.

TEL AVIV, MUSÉE DE TEL AVIV, PAVILLON HELENA RUBINSTEIN. *Rodin*. Exhibition Catalog. February-March, 1967.

Los Angeles County

Board of Supervisors

108

Frank G. Bonelli, *Chairman*
Burton W. Chace
Ernest E. Debs
Warren M. Dorn
Kenneth Hahn
Lindon S. Hollinger,
   Chief Administrative Officer

Los Angeles County Museum of Art

Board of Trustees

Edward W. Carter, *Chairman*
Sidney F. Brody, *President*
William T. Sesnon, Jr. *Vice-President*
Howard Ahmanson, *Vice-President*
Mrs. Aerol Arnold, *Vice-President*
Mrs. Freeman Gates, *Vice-President*
Franklin D. Murphy, *Vice-President*
Mrs. Kellogg Spear, *Secretary*
Theodore E. Cummings
Justin Dart
Charles E. Ducommun
Joseph B. Koepfli
Mrs. Rudolph Liebig
Charles O. Matcham
Henry T. Mudd
Edwin W. Pauley
Taft B. Schreiber
Richard E. Sherwood
Norton Simon
Maynard J. Toll
John Walker
Hal B. Wallis
Mrs. Stuart E. Weaver, Jr.
M. Norvel Young

Director

Kenneth Donahue

INVENTORY 74

LIBRARY
JUNIOR COLLEGE DISTRICT
ST. LOUIS, MO.

FALL 77

INVENTORY 1983

LIBRARY
JUNIOR COLLEGE DISTRICT
ST. LOUIS, MO.